Handwriting

practice made fun

silly sentences

Growing Minds

PRESS

Visit Us Online

Download Free Printables

growingmindspress.wixsite.com/home

Follow us on social media:

Please remember to leave us a review.

SCAN ME

Our Print Handwriting Program

Our print handwriting program is a comprehensive series of five books that includes instructional workbooks with corresponding animated YouTube videos, practice workbooks, and free resources on our website. We use a systematic approach that is outlined on the next few pages.

Book #1: Pre-writing Practice Made Fun: Preschool Writing Activities
Grades: Preschool – Pre-Kindergarten (ages 3-5)

Pre-writing and Fine Motor Skills
With this workbook, preschoolers can practice pre-writing strokes in preparation for letter and number formation. We have intentionally omitted lowercase letters in order to maintain a developmentally appropriate focus on pre-writing strokes, uppercase letters, and numbers. As developing fine motor skills is critical for handwriting success, we provide free resources on our website to assist you in fostering this important area of your child's development. We recommend using small golf size pencils or crayons broken in half to help your preschooler with their grasp while they enjoy this workbook.

Book #2: Handwriting Practice Made Fun: Focus on Formation
Grades: Pre-Kindergarten – 1st Grade (ages 4-7)

A Solid Foundation in Handwriting
Learning letter and number formation is a critical component for a solid foundation in handwriting. This workbook provides important step-by-step instruction presented in a stroke-based teaching order built on developmental progression. We focus on correct handwriting formation so that learners can eventually write letters and numbers with automaticity. We also encourage you to continue using the free and fun fine motor activities on our website for a positive impact on your child's handwriting development.

Our Print Handwriting Program

Animated Lesson Videos

A unique and valuable part of our program is our free animated lesson videos featuring our lovable joke-telling character, Funny Bunny Frankie. These videos bring handwriting to life by demonstrating how each letter and number is formed using simple movements that your child can easily understand. Together, this workbook and the corresponding videos provide a multi-sensory approach that will appeal to all learners.

Letter Reversals or Dyslexia?

We also address the common problem of letter reversals. Many parents believe when they see their child writing letters backwards or upside down that it is indicative of dyslexia. This is a misconception. It is normal for children under the age of 8 to write letters in reverse. With our program, we address letter reversals early, which can prevent the issue from starting or continuing. If your child is age 8 or older and continues to write letters in reverse after specifically addressing letter reversals, then we recommend consulting a professional as it may or may not be related to dyslexia.

Book #3: Handwriting Practice Made Fun: Focus on Size and Placement
Grades: 1st Grade — 3rd Grade (ages 6-9)

Handwriting Size and Placement

The next step in our handwriting program teaches your child how to correctly size and place letters and numbers on handwriting lines. Being aware of how to effectively use the handwriting lines will help your learner improve their handwriting skills. We continue our stroke-based teaching order to reinforce handwriting formation while they build the next progression of skills.

Our Print Handwriting Program

Animated Videos

Our lovable joke-telling friend Funny Bunny Frankie is back in this workbook and in animated videos to introduce his friends the Alpha Buddies. Together they will show your learner how to identify where each letter and number belong on the handwriting lines. These fun videos teach your child the purpose of each line and will keep them engaged while they focus on the size and placement of their handwriting.

Book #4: Handwriting Practice Made Fun: Silly Sentences
Grades: 1st Grade – 4th Grade (ages 6-10)

Letter and Sentence Handwriting Practice

The next workbook in our handwriting series provides letter and sentence practice using sight words. Students will roll a die to select words from lists that will help them build silly sentences. They will copy their silly sentence on handwriting lines and perform self-checks to ensure proper sentence formation. We use a focus letter with each worksheet to provide ample letter practice while also practicing handwriting with sentences. If your child enjoys being silly, they'll enjoy practicing handwriting with this silly and fun workbook.

Book #5: Handwriting Practice Made Fun: Jokes, Riddles, Stories, and More!
Grades: 2nd Grade – 4th Grade (ages 7-10)

Sentence Handwriting Practice

This handwriting practice workbook has a variety of fun activities for tracing and copying sentences. Using jokes, riddles, silly stories, fun facts, and decoding learners will practice handwriting in a fun and engaging way. If your child needs any review, they can watch the appropriate videos from our YouTube channel.

Which Book Should I Choose?

We have provided general placement guidelines by grade and age. Consider your child's skill level and needs when making your decision.

Preschool (ages 3-4)

> #1: Pre-Writing Practice Made Fun: Preschool Writing Activities

Pre-Kindergarten (ages 4-5)

> #1: Pre-Writing Practice Made Fun: Preschool Writing Activities
> OR
> #2: Handwriting Practice Made Fun: Focus on Formation

If you check one or more of the boxes below, choose Book #1. If not, choose Book #2

❑ My child has had little or no prior pre-writing strokes practice (vertical lines, horizontal lines, circle, cross, diagonal lines, square, X, and triangle)

❑ My child needs more pre-writing stokes practice

❑ My child has difficulty with some of the pre-writing strokes

Which Book Should I Choose?

Kindergarten (ages 5-6)

#2: Handwriting Practice Made Fun: Focus on Formation

1st Grade (ages 6-7)

#2: Handwriting Practice Made Fun: Focus on Formation
OR
#3: Handwriting Practice Made Fun: Focus on Size and Placement
OR
#4: Handwriting Practice Made Fun: Silly Sentences

☐ My child needs more help to correctly form letters and numbers (Choose Book #2)

☐ My child forms letters and numbers correctly (Choose Book #3)

☐ My child has finished Book #3 (Choose Book #4)

Which Book Should I Choose?

2nd Grade – 3rd Grade (ages 7-9)

> #3: Handwriting Practice Made Fun: Focus on Size and Placement
> OR
> #4: Handwriting Practice Made Fun: Silly Sentences
> OR
> #5: Handwriting Practice Made Fun: Jokes, Riddles, Stories, and More!

❑ My child needs help to correctly form some letters or numbers (Choose Book #3)

❑ My child needs help to place some letters or numbers correctly on handwriting lines (Choose Book #3)

❑ My child needs both letter and sentence handwriting practice (Choose Book #4)

❑ My child needs just handwriting practice with sentences (Choose Book #5)

4th Grade (ages 9-10)

> #4: Handwriting Practice Made Fun: Silly Sentences
> OR
> #5: Handwriting Practice Made Fun: Jokes, Riddles, Stories, and More!

❑ My child needs both letter and sentence handwriting practice (Choose Book #4)

❑ My child needs just handwriting practice with sentences (Choose Book #5)

Benefits of This Book

✓ Uses sight words for sentence handwriting practice

✓ Fun activity allows learners to roll a die and choose words in order to make a silly sentence

✓ Has a focus letter on every page that is also used in sentence writing for ample letter practice

✓ Reminders for letter placement within handwriting lines help students improve handwriting

✓ Correct letter and number formation with correct directional arrows

✓ Starting positions emphasized for proper handwriting development

✓ Continuous stroke patterns for efficient and fluid handwriting practice

✓ No unnecessary pencil lifting to help avoid awkward stroke order

✓ Self-check sentence reminders reinforce proper sentence formation

How to Make Silly Sentences

ROLL
a die to choose from the word lists

HIGHLIGHT
the chosen words

WRITE
the words to make your sentence

Example:

First Roll

Second Roll

Third Roll

First List
1. A long
2. The red
3. Her happy
4. My fast
5. Our tired
6. This tiny

Second List
1. teacher
2. giraffe
3. nose
4. piano
5. sock
6. tomato

Third List
1. dances at school
2. sings in a library
3. sits under a table
4. runs around a barn
5. climbs over a fence
6. hops with a bunny

Write your *Silly Sentence*.

My fast teacher hops with a bunny.

Handwriting On Three Lines

The three handwriting lines are there to help you know where the letters should go.

top line ➞ ——————————
middle line ➞ - - - - - - - - - - - -
bottom line ➞ ——————————

All of the uppercase letters stay between the <u>top</u> line and the <u>bottom</u> line just like this.

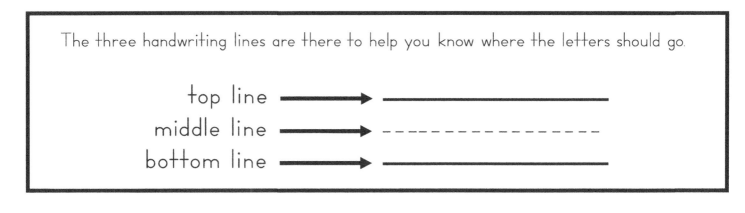

ABCDEFGHIJKLM
NOPQRSTUVWXYZ

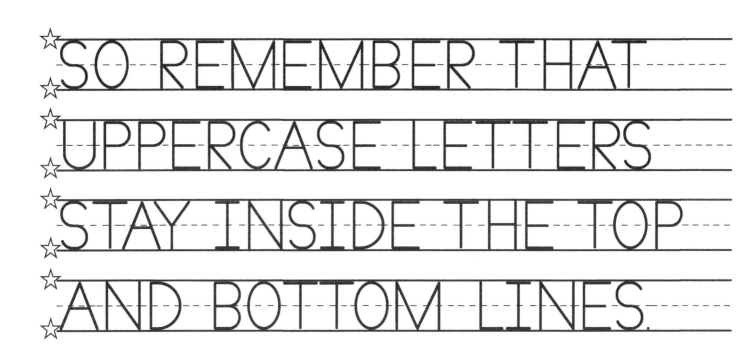

SO REMEMBER THAT
UPPERCASE LETTERS
STAY INSIDE THE TOP
AND BOTTOM LINES.

Handwriting On Three Lines

Tall lowercase letters stay between the <u>top</u> line and the <u>bottom</u> line just like this.

☆
bdfhklt
☆

Short lowercase letters stay between the <u>middle</u> line and the <u>bottom</u> line just like this.

☆
aceimnorsuvwxz
☆

Tail lowercase letters go below the <u>bottom</u> line. They stay between the <u>middle</u> line and a little passed the <u>bottom</u> line just like this.

☆
gjpqy
☆

So remember:

Tall letters go here

Short letters go here

Tail letters go here

Aa Let's Review the Letter

Start with your pencil on the starting dot

Keep A between the <u>top</u> line and <u>bottom</u> line.

<u>Top</u> line ⟶

<u>Bottom</u> line ⟶

Keep a between the <u>middle</u> line and <u>bottom</u> line.

<u>Middle</u> line ⟶

<u>Bottom</u> line ⟶

Trace It

Try It

You Can Do It!

Roll, Highlight, and Write

First List	Second List	Third List
1. A bad	1. hand	1. watched a parade.
2. A clean	2. plane	2. wears pants.
3. A smart	3. face	3. hears a bang.
4. An angry	4. game	4. plants a daisy.
5. A careful	5. avocado	5. calls a teacher.
6. A late	6. animal	6. caught a ball.

Write your **Silly Sentence.**

☐ Starts with capital letter   ☐ Finger spaces between words   ☐ Ends with a punctuation mark

Practice writing your best Aa five times.

Roll, Highlight, and Write

First List	Second List	Third List
1. A beautiful	1. family	1. ate a salad.
2. An important	2. dancer	2. waves to a man.
3. An amazing	3. hat	3. travels with a ball.
4. A famous	4. car	4. draws on a wall.
5. A brave	5. bear	5. ran around a yard.
6. A warm	6. teacher	6. plays with a bat.

Write your **silly sentence.**

☐ Starts with capital letter   ☐ Finger spaces between words   ☐ Ends with a punctuation mark

Practice writing your best Aa five times.

Roll, Highlight, and Write

First List	Second List	Third List
1. A rabbit	1. walks	1. all over a machine.
2. An apple	2. paints	2. above a table.
3. A cake	3. dances	3. at a park.
4. Santa Claus	4. races	4. near an ocean.
5. A baby	5. eats	5. across a yard.
6. A head	6. cleans	6. around a bank.

Write your *Silly Sentence*.

☐ Starts with capital letter   ☐ Finger spaces between words   ☐ Ends with a punctuation mark

Practice writing your best Aa five times.

Aa Make Your Own Sentence

Who	What	Where
An apple	ate an avocado	at a race.
An ant	made a cake	above the earth
An aunt	watched T.V.	across the road.
An astronaut	plays a game	around the sea.
An airplane	falls asleep	away at camp.
An acorn	reads a book	aboard a train.

Write your **Silly Sentence.**

_____

- -

_____

- -

_____

- -

_____

- -

_____

☐ Starts with capital letter   ☐ Finger spaces between words   ☐ Ends with a punctuation mark

Practice writing your best Aa five times.

Aa -

Copy and Draw

Copy your favorite **Silly Sentence** from the Aa pages. Then draw it below.

_____

- -

_____

- -

_____

- -

_____

- -

_____

☐ Starts with capital letter   ☐ Finger spaces between words   ☐ Ends with a punctuation mark

Practice writing your best Aa five times.

B b Let's Review the Letter

Start with your pencil on the starting dot

Keep B between the top line and bottom line.

Top line ──────▶

Bottom line ──────▶

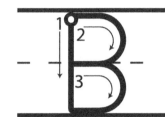

Keep b between the top line and bottom line.

Top line ──────▶

Bottom line ──────▶

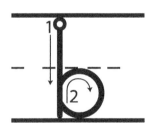

Trace It   Try It

B b   - - - - - -   You Can Do It!

Roll, Highlight, and Write

First List	Second List	Third List
1. A beautiful	1. bear	1. barked at a bench.
2. The blue	2. butterfly	2. became a beach.
3. Her busy	3. bread	3. brushed a beard.
4. His bossy	4. boots	4. bolted into a barn.
5. This bad	5. bike	5. bounced on a bush.
6. That black	6. button	6. baked a basket.

Write your *Silly Sentence.*

☐ Starts with capital letter ☐ Finger spaces between words ☐ Ends with a punctuation mark

Practice writing your best Bb five times.

Roll, Highlight, and Write

First List	Second List	Third List
1. A bright	1. balloon	1. borrows a bow.
2. Our broken	2. bed	2. buried a bone.
3. The brilliant	3. bus	3. observed a birthday
4. That bad	4. banana	4. began to bowl.
5. This bored	5. broom	5. bounces on a bridge.
6. A bold	6. bee	6. belonged to a boy.

Write your **Silly Sentence.**

☐ Starts with capital letter   ☐ Finger spaces between words   ☐ Ends with a punctuation mark

Practice writing your best Bb five times.

Roll, Highlight, and Write

First List	Second List	Third List
1. A bat	1. blocked	1. a basement.
2. The baby	2. buys	2. a bun.
3. This berry	3. bothered	3. a bug.
4. That bubble	4. bumped	4. a bucket.
5. This boy	5. builds	5. a breakfast.
6. A belly	6. believed in	6. a buddy.

Write your *Silly sentence.*

☐ Starts with capital letter   ☐ Finger spaces between words   ☐ Ends with a punctuation mark

Practice writing your best Bb five times.

Bb Make Your Own Sentence

Who	What	Where
A bird	bought a book	beside a bed.
Her brother	broke a branch	between a bun.
The boat	bit a bone	behind a bank.
Our bus	built a bell	by a business.
His brain	bent a box	below a bridge.
That ball	balanced a block	by a beach.

Write your *silly sentence*.

_____

- - - - - - - - - - - - - - - - - - -

_____

- - - - - - - - - - - - - - - - - - -

_____

- - - - - - - - - - - - - - - - - - -

_____

- - - - - - - - - - - - - - - - - - -

_____

☐ Starts with capital letter   ☐ Finger spaces between words   ☐ Ends with a punctuation mark

Practice writing your best Bb five times.

Bb

Copy and Draw

Copy your favorite **SILLY SENTENCE** from the Bb pages. Then draw it below.

☐ Starts with capital letter   ☐ Finger spaces between words   ☐ Ends with a punctuation mark

Practice writing your best Bb five times.

Cc **Let's Review the Letter**

Start with your pencil on the starting dot

Keep C between the <u>top</u> line and <u>bottom</u> line.

<u>Top</u> line ➡

<u>Bottom</u> line ➡

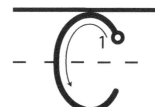

Keep c between the <u>middle</u> line and <u>bottom</u> line.

<u>Middle</u> line ➡

<u>Bottom</u> line ➡

Trace It   Try It

You Can Do It!

Roll, Highlight, and Write

First List	Second List	Third List
1. A chilly	1. can	1. cooked carrots.
2. The crabby	2. cat	2. cheered in a crowd.
3. Her clay	3. clown	3. created cards.
4. That calm	4. customer	4. chewed candy.
5. My comfy	5. chef	5. colored a coat.
6. A clumsy	6. clam	6. cleaned a car.

Write your **silly sentence.**

_____

- -

_____

- -

_____

- -

_____

- -

_____

- -

_____

☐ Starts with capital letter   ☐ Finger spaces between words   ☐ Ends with a punctuation mark

Practice writing your best Cc five times.

Cc

Cc

Roll, Highlight, and Write

First List	Second List	Third List
1. A cranky	1. chicken	1. cut a card
2. His cold	2. chair	2. checked a clue
3. The cozy	3. cow	3. changed coats
4. This cheery	4. circle	4. combs a cat
5. That crazy	5. corn	5. touched a rock
6. A clean	6. calendar	6. covered a couch

Write your **silly sentence.**

☐ Starts with capital letter   ☐ Finger spaces between words   ☐ Ends with a punctuation mark

Practice writing your best Cc five times.

Cc

Roll, Highlight, and Write

First List	Second List	Third List
1. A crawling	1. cube	1. camps in a cabin.
2. The crafty	2. clock	2. carried a computer
3. The chatty	3. cup	3. clings to a chair.
4. A cloudy	4. crab	4. chomps on a cookie
5. That clear	5. cat	5. climbs a canyon.
6. A crazy	6. calf	6. claps for a car.

Write your **silly sentence.**

☐ Starts with capital letter   ☐ Finger spaces between words   ☐ Ends with a punctuation mark

Practice writing your best Cc five times.

Cc

Make Your Own Sentence

Who	What	Where
That cake	cooked a can	close to the country.
His cat	called a cab	across the ocean.
Her child	caught a chicken	located in a city.
A car	carried a couch	stuck in space.
The cloud	closed a cabin	back in a corner.
This church	climbed a crib	across a crowd.

Write your **Silly Sentence.**

☐ Starts with capital letter ☐ Finger spaces between words ☐ Ends with a punctuation mark

Practice writing your best Cc five times.

Copy and Draw

Copy your favorite **Silly Sentence** from the Cc pages. Then draw it below.

☐ Starts with capital letter   ☐ Finger spaces between words   ☐ Ends with a punctuation mark

Practice writing your best Cc five times.

Cc

Dd Let's Review the Letter

Start with your pencil on the starting dot

Keep D between the top line and bottom line.

Top line ➔

Bottom line ➔

Keep d between the top line and bottom line.

Top line ➔

Bottom line ➔

Trace It

Try It

You Can Do It!

Roll, Highlight, and Write

First List	Second List	Third List
1. A kind	1. duck	1. needs a doughnut
2. The red	2. dog	2. fed a donkey
3. My good	3. dancer	3. jumped over a ditch
4. An old	4. driver	4. passed a doorway
5. The hard	5. dolphin	5. picked up a dime
6. An afraid	6. dandelion	6. read a dictionary

Write your **silly sentence.**

☐ Starts with capital letter   ☐ Finger spaces between words   ☐ Ends with a punctuation mark

Practice writing your best Dd five times.

Dd

Roll, Highlight, and Write

First List	Second List	Third List
1. A daring	1. president	1. lifted a fridge.
2. The gold	2. lady	2. rolled two dice.
3. My cold	3. head	3. smiled at a dentist.
4. A bored	4. bed	4. builds a bridge.
5. The dizzy	5. student	5. biked on a road.
6. A loud	6. friend	6. finds a dollar.

Write your **Silly Sentence.**

☐ Starts with capital letter   ☐ Finger spaces between words   ☐ Ends with a punctuation mark

Practice writing your best Dd five times.

Roll, Highlight, and Write

First List	Second List	Third List
1. This kid	1. made a video	1. inside a drawer.
2. My dog	2. sewed a dress	2. down a drain.
3. A seed	3. sends a card	3. during the day.
4. My bird	4. made a bed	4. outside a building
5. A drum	5. had dessert	5. behind a garden.
6. A dime	6. drops a dish	6. beside a friend.

Write your **Silly Sentence.**

☐ Starts with capital letter   ☐ Finger spaces between words   ☐ Ends with a punctuation mark

Practice writing your best Dd five times.

Make Your Own Sentence

Who	What	Where
A door	dries dishes	at a diner.
The doctor	draws doughnuts	downstairs.
My dad	dashed	inside a dungeon.
A dinosaur	dreams	across a pond.
Her doll	danced	down the road.
Our dog	drives	on an island.

Write your **silly sentence.**

☐ Starts with capital letter   ☐ Finger spaces between words   ☐ Ends with a punctuation mark

Practice writing your best Dd five times.

Dd

Copy and Draw

Copy your favorite **Silly Sentence** from the Dd pages. Then draw it below.

☐ Starts with capital letter   ☐ Finger spaces between words   ☐ Ends with a punctuation mark

Practice writing your best Dd five times.

Ee # Let's Review the Letter

Start with your pencil on the starting dot

Keep E between the <u>top</u> line and <u>bottom</u> line.

<u>Top</u> line ➜

<u>Bottom</u> line ➜

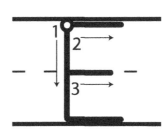

Keep e between the <u>middle</u> line and <u>bottom</u> line.

<u>Middle</u> line ➜

<u>Bottom</u> line ➜

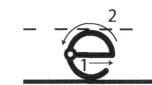

Trace It

Try It

You Can Do It!

Roll, Highlight, and Write

First List	Second List	Third List
1. The eager	1. nose	1. enjoys everything.
2. An empty	2. person	2. feels great.
3. An epic	3. insect	3. returns a package.
4. The extra	4. wheel	4. receives a letter.
5. An excited	5. planet	5. measures a table.
6. An excellent	6. egg	6. waved excitedly.

Write your *silly sentence.*

_____

- -

_____

_____

- -

_____

_____

- -

_____

_____

- -

_____

☐ Starts with capital letter   ☐ Finger spaces between words   ☐ Ends with a punctuation mark

Practice writing your best Ee five times.

Ee _____

Ee

Roll, Highlight, and Write

First List	Second List	Third List
1. Our yellow	1. paper	1. helps a nurse.
2. The heavy	2. nest	2. rests in bed.
3. A whole	3. horse	3. grew tired.
4. An exciting	4. plane	4. sent an e-mail.
5. My little	5. bell	5. wears shoes.
6. This large	6. instrument	6. echoed a voice.

Write your **Silly Sentence.**

_____

_____

_____

_____

☐ Starts with capital letter   ☐ Finger spaces between words   ☐ Ends with a punctuation mark

Practice writing your best Ee five times.

Ee _____

Roll, Highlight, and Write

First List	Second List	Third List
1. An apple	1. jumped	1. in a basement.
2. The giraffe	2. sleeps	2. under a tree.
3. My shoe	3. worked	3. before breakfast
4. His leg	4. cooked	4. inside a store.
5. Her rose	5. played	5. at the beach.
6. Our team	6. fell	6. above a plane.

Write your *Silly Sentence.*

☐ Starts with capital letter   ☐ Finger spaces between words   ☐ Ends with a punctuation mark

Practice writing your best Ee five times.

Make Your Own Sentence

Ee

Who
An engineer
That elf
The elk
This engine
My ear
An envelope

What
eats an egg
sees a lake
takes a test
washed clothes
opens a present
ties a shoe

Where
in a maze.
at the office.
in the winter.
at home.
on an escalator.
in a puddle.

Write your **Silly Sentence**.

☐ Starts with capital letter   ☐ Finger spaces between words   ☐ Ends with a punctuation mark

Practice writing your best Ee five times.

Ee

Copy and Draw

Copy your favorite **Silly Sentence** from the Ee pages. Then draw it below.

_____

- - - - - - - - - - - - - - - - - - - -
_____

_____

- - - - - - - - - - - - - - - - - - - -
_____

_____

- - - - - - - - - - - - - - - - - - - -
_____

☐ Starts with capital letter   ☐ Finger spaces between words   ☐ Ends with a punctuation mark

Practice writing your best Ee five times.

E e

Ff # Let's Review the Letter

Start with your pencil on the starting dot

Keep F between the <u>top</u> line and <u>bottom</u> line.

<u>Top</u> line ➡️

<u>Bottom</u> line ➡️

Keep f between the <u>top</u> line and <u>bottom</u> line.

<u>Top</u> line ➡️

<u>Bottom</u> line ➡️

Trace It

Try It

You Can Do It!

Roll, Highlight, and Write

First List	Second List	Third List
1. A full	1. fort	1. freezes an office.
2. The firm	2. foot	2. felt frustrated.
3. Our frozen	3. frog	3. finds a golf ball.
4. My favorite	4. friend	4. fixed the frosting.
5. His funny	5. family	5. lifted a freezer.
6. Her fancy	6. waffle	6. fits flip flops.

Write your *silly sentence.*

_____

_____

_____

_____

_____

☐ Starts with capital letter   ☐ Finger spaces between words   ☐ Ends with a punctuation mark

Practice writing your best Ff five times.

Roll, Highlight, and Write

First List	Second List	Third List
1. A fabulous	1. fence	1. found a flea.
2. The furry	2. fawn	2. fights a firefly.
3. His frosty	3. floor	3. fetched food.
4. My fluffy	4. flower	4. folded a flag.
5. Our soft	5. fox	5. falls forward.
6. Her flat	6. fish	6. fled a farm.

Write your *Silly Sentence.*

_____

_____

_____

_____

_____

_____

_____

☐ Starts with capital letter   ☐ Finger spaces between words   ☐ Ends with a punctuation mark

Practice writing your best Ff five times.

First List	Second List	Third List
1. My fun	1. face	1. followed a fox.
2. A flying	2. fork	2. flees a field.
3. The fragile	3. finger	3. fished for food.
4. A former	4. flamingo	4. feels fancy.
5. A frowning	5. fly	5. fixed a fiddle.
6. A fake	6. flag	6. feared a fog.

Write your *Silly Sentence.*

☐ Starts with capital letter   ☐ Finger spaces between words   ☐ Ends with a punctuation mark

Practice writing your best Ff five times.

Ff Make Your Own Sentence

Who	What	Where
Our fruit	flew with a flamingo	on a roof.
My family	flipped a fork	from a field.
A farmer	fell forward	on a fishing boat.
His father	flexes fingers	at a fair.
A flower	finds four foxes	far from France.
That fish	flapped with a fish	in a fairy tale.

Write your **Silly Sentence.**

_____

- -

_____

- -

_____

- -

_____

- -

_____

- -

☐ Starts with capital letter   ☐ Finger spaces between words   ☐ Ends with a punctuation mark

Practice writing your best Ff five times.

Copy and Draw

Copy your favorite *Silly Sentence* from the Ff pages. Then draw it below.

☐ Starts with capital letter   ☐ Finger spaces between words   ☐ Ends with a punctuation mark

Practice writing your best Ff five times.

Gg Let's Review the Letter

Start with your pencil on the starting dot

Keep G between the <u>top</u> line and <u>bottom</u> line.

<u>Top</u> line ➔

<u>Bottom</u> line ➔

Keep g between the <u>middle</u> line and <u>a little passed the bottom</u> line.

<u>Middle</u> line ➔

<u>A little passed the bottom</u> line ➔

Trace It

Try It

You Can Do It!

Roll, Highlight, and Write

First List	Second List	Third List
1. A giggly	1. guest	1. grabbed grass
2. This glad	2. gorilla	2. gives a gift
3. The greedy	3. giraffe	3. guided a group
4. A greasy	4. giant	4. gazed at Grandma
5. A grouchy	5. grape	5. grows a garden
6. Our gifted	6. glove	6. gulped garlic

Write your *Silly Sentence.*

_____

- -

_____

- -

_____

- -

_____

- -

_____

☐ Starts with capital letter   ☐ Finger spaces between words   ☐ Ends with a punctuation mark

Practice writing your best Gg five times.

Gg

Gg Roll, Highlight, and Write

First List	Second List	Third List
1. That young	1. germ	1. glared at a goat
2. The long	2. gopher	2. gives a king a ring.
3. A good	3. ghost	3. sings a song.
4. Our strong	4. pig	4. gathered wigs.
5. A green	5. ring	5. grilled a burger.
6. This goofy	6. leg	6. glides on a glacier.

Write your **silly sentence.**

☐ Starts with capital letter   ☐ Finger spaces between words   ☐ Ends with a punctuation mark

Practice writing your best Gg five times.

Gg

Roll, Highlight, and Write

First List	Second List	Third List
1. That gnu	1. galloped	1. during spring.
2. Our dog	2. wiggled	2. along a gate.
3. The girl	3. sang	3. during a golf game.
4. A glass	4. zig zags	4. while getting gold.
5. This guitar	5. grinned	5. at a wedding.
6. Our group	6. golfs	6. with a gator.

Write your **Silly Sentence**.

_____

_____

_____

_____

_____

_____

☐ Starts with capital letter   ☐ Finger spaces between words   ☐ Ends with a punctuation mark

Practice writing your best Gg five times.

G g _____

Gg Make Your Own Sentence

Who	What	Where
My gift	glued a page	along the galaxy.
A gem	glows brightly	in the grass.
A goat	hugs a giant	through a gate.
A girl	growled angrily	at gym class.
My game	grips a gorilla	along the highway.
A gear	gulped grapes	in a garage.

Write your **Silly Sentence.**

☐ Starts with capital letter   ☐ Finger spaces between words   ☐ Ends with a punctuation mark

Practice writing your best Gg five times.

Gg

Copy and Draw

Copy your favorite **Silly Sentence** from the Gg pages. Then draw it below.

☐ Starts with capital letter ☐ Finger spaces between words ☐ Ends with a punctuation mark

Practice writing your best Gg five times.

Gg

Let's Review the Letter

Start with your pencil on the starting dot

Keep H between the <u>top</u> line and <u>bottom</u> line.

<u>Top</u> line ➡️

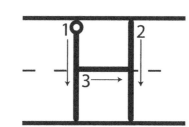

<u>Bottom</u> line ➡️

Keep h between the <u>top</u> line and <u>bottom</u> line.

<u>Top</u> line ➡️

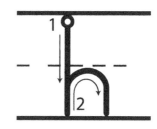

<u>Bottom</u> line ➡️

Trace It

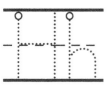

Try It

You Can Do It!

Roll, Highlight, and Write

First List	Second List	Third List
1. Our happy	1. hill	1. hugged a hen.
2. A hungry	2. hand	2. has a helicopter.
3. That hot	3. hat	3. heard a harp.
4. The heavy	4. ham	4. helped a hippo.
5. A handsome	5. house	5. hit a hockey puck.
6. This hazy	6. hexagon	6. hid an acorn.

Write your **Silly Sentence**.

_____

- -

_____

- -

_____

- -

_____

- -

_____

- -

☐ Starts with capital letter   ☐ Finger spaces between words   ☐ Ends with a punctuation mark

Practice writing your best Hh five times.

Roll, Highlight, and Write

First List	Second List	Third List
1. This hurt	1. wheel	1. visits a neighbor.
2. A shocked	2. mouth	2. changed a machine.
3. The heroic	3. head	3. reached a hill.
4. Our shy	4. horse	4. washed a dish.
5. Her bright	5. father	5. marched at school.
6. A fresh	6. sheep	6. finishes homework.

Write your **Silly Sentence.**

_____

- -

_____

- -

_____

- -

_____

- -

_____

- -

_____

☐ Starts with capital letter   ☐ Finger spaces between words   ☐ Ends with a punctuation mark

Practice writing your best Hh five times.

Roll, Highlight, and Write

First List	Second List	Third List
1. A fish	1. held a hand	1. during a holiday.
2. A horse	2. buys a hen	2. in a neighborhood
3. A chair	3. hid clothes	3. without a hand.
4. A head	4. hears a harp	4. with a hamburger
5. A mother	5. hugs a chair	5. within a house.
6. A shape	6. felt healthy	6. with a hotdog.

Write your **Silly Sentence.**

_____

- -

_____

- -

_____

- -

_____

- -

_____

☐ Starts with capital letter   ☐ Finger spaces between words   ☐ Ends with a punctuation mark

Practice writing your best Hh five times.

Make Your Own Sentence

Hh

Who	What	Where
A hippo	hurries	beneath a ship.
Our hero	hiccups	behind a shop.
A hedgehog	hummed	underneath a branch.
A human	hopped	through a church.
Her heart	honked	behind a hill.
My hair	hiked	through a highway.

Write your **Silly Sentence.**

☐ Starts with capital letter ☐ Finger spaces between words ☐ Ends with a punctuation mark

Practice writing your best Hh five times.

Copy and Draw

Copy your favorite **Silly Sentence** from the Hh pages. Then draw it below.

_____

- -

_____

- -

_____

- -

_____

☐ Starts with capital letter   ☐ Finger spaces between words   ☐ Ends with a punctuation mark

Practice writing your best Hh five times.

Ii # Let's Review the Letter

Keep I between the <u>top</u> line and <u>bottom</u> line.

<u>Top</u> line ⟶

<u>Bottom</u> line ⟶

Keep i between the <u>middle</u> line and <u>bottom</u> line.

<u>Middle</u> line ⟶

<u>Bottom</u> line ⟶

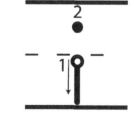

Trace It   Try It

You Can Do It!

Roll, Highlight, and Write

First List	Second List	Third List
1. That quick	1. chair	1. listens to music.
2. An injured	2. prize	2. sings with a piano
3. An itchy	3. train	3. tied a string.
4. The ideal	4. ring	4. trips on a stick
5. An intelligent	5. king	5. sits still.
6. An indigo	6. pencil	6. picks a fruit.

Write your **silly sentence.**

_____
- -
_____
- -
_____
- -
_____
- -
_____
- -
_____

☐ Starts with capital letter   ☐ Finger spaces between words   ☐ Ends with a punctuation mark

Practice writing your best Ii five times.

Roll, Highlight, and Write

First List	Second List	Third List
1. An important	1. fish	1. fills a sink.
2. An interesting	2. kitty	2. fixes a kite.
3. An intense	3. scientist	3. visits a pit.
4. An icy	4. triangle	4. arrives in Italy.
5. An icky	5. pizza	5. stirs a drink.
6. A silent	6. lion	6. lives in a city.

Write your **Silly Sentence**.

_____

- - - - - - - - - - - - - - - - -

_____

- - - - - - - - - - - - - - - - -

_____

- - - - - - - - - - - - - - - - -

_____

- - - - - - - - - - - - - - - - -

_____

- - - - - - - - - - - - - - - - -

_____

☐ Starts with capital letter   ☐ Finger spaces between words   ☐ Ends with a punctuation mark

Practice writing your best Ii five times.

I i

Roll, Highlight, and Write

Ii

First List	Second List	Third List
1. An icicle	1. lifts weights	1. at night
2. A pig	2. invents an item	2. in the air
3. A lid	3. hid a cookie	3. during spring
4. A giant	4. gave a ride	4. inside an engine
5. A tiger	5. invites a friend	5. during a holiday
6. A snail	6. finds a wig	6. on a swing

Write your *Silly Sentence.*

_____

- -

_____

- -

_____

- -

_____

- -

_____

☐ Starts with capital letter   ☐ Finger spaces between words   ☐ Ends with a punctuation mark

Practice writing your best Ii five times.

Ii

Make Your Own Sentence

Who	What	Where
An ice cream	licks icing	on an island.
An insect	swims	inside an igloo.
An instrument	irons a shirt	in India.
An infant	inflates a tire	beside a river.
An ice cube	instructs kids	behind a hill.
An iguana	rides a bike	on a ship.

Write your **Silly Sentence.**

☐ Starts with capital letter   ☐ Finger spaces between words   ☐ Ends with a punctuation mark

Practice writing your best Ii five times.

Copy and Draw

Copy your favorite **SiLLY SenTence** from the Ii pages. Then draw it below.

☐ Starts with capital letter   ☐ Finger spaces between words   ☐ Ends with a punctuation mark

Practice writing your best Ii five times.

JⱼJj # Let's Review the Letter

Start with your pencil on the starting dot

Keep J between the <u>top</u> line and <u>bottom</u> line.

<u>Top</u> line ➡️

<u>Bottom</u> line ➡️

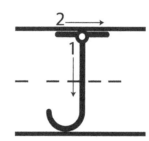

Keep j between the <u>middle</u> line and <u>a little</u> <u>passed the bottom</u> line.

<u>Middle</u> line ➡️

<u>A little passed</u> <u>the bottom</u> line ➡️

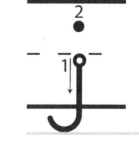

Trace It

Try It

You Can Do It!

Roll, Highlight, and Write

First List	Second List	Third List
1. A joyful	1. jacket	1. jumps on an object
2. An injured	2. fajita	2. joined a job.
3. A jumbled	3. janitor	3. enjoyed a jog.
4. A jinxed	4. jet	4. jotted in a journal
5. The jagged	5. judge	5. adjusts a banjo.
6. That jumbo	6. journalist	6. jinxed a ninja.

Write your **Silly Sentence**.

_____

- -

_____

- -

_____

- -

_____

- -

_____

- -

_____

☐ Starts with capital letter   ☐ Finger spaces between words   ☐ Ends with a punctuation mark

Practice writing your best Jj five times.

Roll, Highlight, and Write

First List	Second List	Third List
1. A joyful	1. jug	1. jutted out of a jar.
2. An injured	2. jewel	2. enjoyed a joke.
3. A jumbled	3. jellyfish	3. joined a joyride.
4. A jinxed	4. juice	4. jumps over a jeep.
5. The jagged	5. jet ski	5. adjusts a banjo.
6. That jumbo	6. jaw	6. jinxed a ninja.

Write your **Silly Sentence.**

☐ Starts with capital letter ☐ Finger spaces between words ☐ Ends with a punctuation mark

Practice writing your best Jj five times.

Roll, Highlight, and Write

First List	Second List	Third List
1. That jar	1. jogs	1. in a junkyard
2. A juggler	2. jolted	2. on Jupiter.
3. A jackal	3. ejects	3. in the jungle.
4. A jaguar	4. juggles	4. with a jetpack
5. This ninja	5. jingled	5. in Japan.
6. The blue jay	6. injects	6. on a journey.

Write your *Silly Sentence.*

_____

- - - - - - - - - - - - - - - - - - - -

_____

- - - - - - - - - - - - - - - - - - - -

_____

- - - - - - - - - - - - - - - - - - - -

_____

- - - - - - - - - - - - - - - - - - - -

_____

- - - - - - - - - - - - - - - - - - - -

_____

☐ Starts with capital letter   ☐ Finger spaces between words   ☐ Ends with a punctuation mark

Practice writing your best Jj five times.

Make Your Own Sentence

J j

Who	What	Where
That jar	jogs	in a junkyard.
A juggler	jolted	on Jupiter.
A jackal	ejects	in the jungle.
A jaguar	juggles	with a jetpack.
This ninja	jingled	in Japan.
The blue jay	injects	on a journey.

Write your **silly sentence.**

☐ Starts with capital letter ☐ Finger spaces between words ☐ Ends with a punctuation mark

Practice writing your best Jj five times.

J j

Copy and Draw

Copy your favorite **Silly Sentence** from the Jj pages. Then draw it below.

☐ Starts with capital letter   ☐ Finger spaces between words   ☐ Ends with a punctuation mark

Practice writing your best Jj five times.

Kk **Let's Review the Letter**

Start with your pencil on the starting dot

Keep K between the <u>top</u> line and <u>bottom</u> line.

<u>Top</u> line   →

<u>Bottom</u> line   →

Keep k between the <u>top</u> line and <u>bottom</u> line.

<u>Top</u> line   →

<u>Bottom</u> line   →

Trace It   Try It

You Can Do It!

Roll, Highlight, and Write

First List
1. Our kind
2. My keen
3. A joking
4. A quick
5. The shaking
6. That pink

Second List
1. key
2. king
3. kitty
4. kite
5. kid
6. koala

Third List
1. keeps a keyboard
2. knows a knight.
3. knits a sock.
4. kicks a kickball.
5. cooks ketchup.
6. likes a cake.

Write your *silly sentence.*

☐ Starts with capital letter   ☐ Finger spaces between words   ☐ Ends with a punctuation mark

Practice writing your best Kk five times.

Roll, Highlight, and Write

First List	Second List	Third List
1. A weak	1. kangaroo	1. takes a fork.
2. A black	2. kiwi	2. woke a duck.
3. A broken	3. milk	3. makes a knot.
4. A dark	4. rock	4. locked a desk
5. An icky	5. donkey	5. kicks a hockey puck.
6. A wonky	6. chicken	6. honks at a truck.

Write your **Silly Sentence.**

_____

- -

_____

- -

_____

- -

_____

- -

_____

- -

☐ Starts with capital letter   ☐ Finger spaces between words   ☐ Ends with a punctuation mark

Practice writing your best Kk five times.

Roll, Highlight, and Write

First List	Second List	Third List
1. A duck	1. took a sock	1. on a bike.
2. A worker	2. walks quickly	2. on a hike.
3. A stick	3. looks at a clock	3. with a sack.
4. A chick	4. drinks milk	4. in a truck.
5. A book	5. thanks a king	5. in a shack.
6. A cake	6. quacks at a yak	6. with a flock.

Write your **silly sentence.**

☐ Starts with capital letter   ☐ Finger spaces between words   ☐ Ends with a punctuation mark

Practice writing your best Kk five times.

K k

Make Your Own Sentence

Kk

Who	What	Where
This truck	breaks a kite	at a lake.
A cook	bakes a cake	at a park.
My drink	works on a bike	at a party.
Her block	licks a stick	at a bank.
His chalk	likes a koala	in the sky.
That donkey	cracks jokes	on a deck.

Write your *Silly Sentence.*

_____

- - - - - - - - - - - - - - - - -

_____

- - - - - - - - - - - - - - - - -

_____

- - - - - - - - - - - - - - - - -

_____

- - - - - - - - - - - - - - - - -

☐ Starts with capital letter   ☐ Finger spaces between words   ☐ Ends with a punctuation mark

Practice writing your best Kk five times.

Kk

Copy and Draw

Copy your favorite *silly sentence* from the Kk pages. Then draw it below.

☐ Starts with capital letter   ☐ Finger spaces between words   ☐ Ends with a punctuation mark

Practice writing your best Kk five times.

Let's Review the Letter

Start with your pencil on the starting dot

Keep L between the <u>top</u> line and <u>bottom</u> line.

<u>Top</u> line ➔

<u>Bottom</u> line ➔

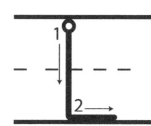

Keep I between the <u>top</u> line and <u>bottom</u> line.

<u>Top</u> line ➔

<u>Bottom</u> line ➔

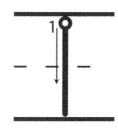

Trace It

Try It

You Can Do It!

Roll, Highlight, and Write

First List	Second List	Third List
1. The little	1. leg	1. laughs in a class.
2. A lost	2. letter	2. leads a line.
3. This long	3. lady	3. learns letters.
4. That loud	4. list	4. spells in English
5. Our lively	5. lion	5. lifts a wall.
6. A late	6. tool	6. likes an apple.

Write your **silly sentence.**

☐ Starts with capital letter   ☐ Finger spaces between words   ☐ Ends with a punctuation mark

Practice writing your best Ll five times.

Roll, Highlight, and Write

First List	Second List	Third List
1. An early	1. table	1. walks for miles
2. The large	2. uncle	2. clashes cymbals
3. Her small	3. animal	3. climbs a ladder
4. That old	4. bell	4. colors a placemat
5. His silent	5. lemon	5. helps a child
6. A lovely	6. doll	6. smells flowers

Write your **silly sentence.**

☐ Starts with capital letter   ☐ Finger spaces between words   ☐ Ends with a punctuation mark

Practice writing your best Ll five times.

Roll, Highlight, and Write

First List	Second List	Third List
1. His apple	1. calls people	1. in a plane.
2. Her ball	2. smiles at a mule	2. at a mall.
3. My class	3. built a plan	3. on the field.
4. The clothes	4. cleans a table	4. over a hill
5. A child	5. learns the rules	5. in a village.
6. The flower	6. listens to a lady	6. in a school.

Write your *Silly Sentence.*

☐ Starts with capital letter   ☐ Finger spaces between words   ☐ Ends with a punctuation mark

Practice writing your best Ll five times.

Make Your Own Sentence

Who	What	Where
The cloud	held a lizard	on a planet.
A dollar	blows a bubble	on the floor.
My family	feels a llama	on an island.
A fly	held a ball	in the world.
That girl	looks at a lion	in a lake.
That syllable	filled fuel	on a wall.

Write your **Silly Sentence.**

☐ Starts with capital letter ☐ Finger spaces between words ☐ Ends with a punctuation mark

Practice writing your best Ll five times.

Copy and Draw

Copy your favorite **Silly Sentence** from the Ll pages. Then draw it below.

☐ Starts with capital letter   ☐ Finger spaces between words   ☐ Ends with a punctuation mark

Practice writing your best Ll five times.

Mm Let's Review the Letter

Start with your pencil on the starting dot

Keep M between the <u>top</u> line and <u>bottom</u> line.

<u>Top</u> line ➡

<u>Bottom</u> line ➡

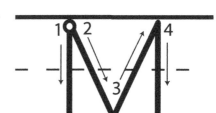

Keep m between the <u>middle</u> line and <u>bottom</u> line.

<u>Middle</u> line ➡

<u>Bottom</u> line ➡

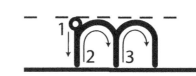

Trace It   Try It

You Can Do It!

Roll, Highlight, and Write

First List	Second List	Third List
1. The main	1. machine	1. makes money.
2. A mad	2. man	2. marched a mile.
3. A mellow	3. monkey	3. mopped a mess.
4. The small	4. meat	4. moved mountains.
5. A modern	5. map	5. measures mats.
6. A merry	6. mug	6. misses mom.

Write your *Silly Sentence.*

_____

- -

_____

- -

_____

- -

_____

- -

_____

- -

☐ Starts with capital letter   ☐ Finger spaces between words   ☐ Ends with a punctuation mark

Practice writing your best Mm five times.

Mm

 # Roll, Highlight, and Write

First List	Second List	Third List
1. A major	1. mat	1. made music.
2. The same	2. family	2. melted metal.
3. A simple	3. monkey	3. mashed mangos.
4. A warm	4. magician	4. climbed a mountain
5. A famous	5. room	5. moves a house.
6. A common	6. animal	6. makes masks.

Write your *Silly Sentence.*

_____

_____

_____

_____

_____

☐ Starts with capital letter ☐ Finger spaces between words ☐ Ends with a punctuation mark

Practice writing your best Mm five times.

Mm

Roll, Highlight, and Write

First List	Second List	Third List
1. My mom	1. swims	1. in a home.
2. A human	2. jumps	2. in America.
3. The woman	3. rhymes	3. at the gym.
4. A number	4. moves	4. over the moon.
5. My arm	5. camps	5. in the mud.
6. An army	6. zooms	6. in summer.

Write your *Silly Sentence*.

☐ Starts with capital letter   ☐ Finger spaces between words   ☐ Ends with a punctuation mark

Practice writing your best Mm five times.

Mm Make Your Own Sentence

Who	What	Where
My mom	makes jam	in a stream.
A mouth	makes meals	in a maze.
Our money	made magic	on a farm.
The moon	smells an animal	at a mall.
This music	made macaroni	on a mountain.
That milk	filmed a movie	at home.

Write your *Silly Sentence*.

_____

- - - - - - - - - - - - - - - - -

_____

- - - - - - - - - - - - - - - - -

_____

- - - - - - - - - - - - - - - - -

_____

- - - - - - - - - - - - - - - - -

_____

☐ Starts with capital letter   ☐ Finger spaces between words   ☐ Ends with a punctuation mark

Practice writing your best Mm five times.

Mm

Copy and Draw

Copy your favorite *SILLY SENTENCE* from the Mm pages. Then draw it below.

☐ Starts with capital letter   ☐ Finger spaces between words   ☐ Ends with a punctuation mark

Practice writing your best Mm five times.

Nn Let's Review the Letter

Start with your pencil on the starting dot

Keep N between the <u>top</u> line and <u>bottom</u> line.

<u>Top</u> line ⟶

<u>Bottom</u> line ⟶

Keep n between the <u>middle</u> line and <u>bottom</u> line.

<u>Middle</u> line ⟶

<u>Bottom</u> line ⟶

Trace It

Try It

You Can Do It!

Roll, Highlight, and Write

First List	Second List	Third List
1. This noisy	1. nest	1. noticed a napkin
2. A natural	2. ninja	2. nods at nobody
3. A nearby	3. niece	3. naps in the winter
4. That new	4. nose	4. nabs a net
5. The green	5. nickel	5. nudged a nephew
6. This tiny	6. newspaper	6. needs a nurse

Write your *Silly Sentence.*

☐ Starts with capital letter   ☐ Finger spaces between words   ☐ Ends with a punctuation mark

Practice writing your best Nn five times.

First List	Second List	Third List
1. A funny	1. king	1. prints notes.
2. That kind	2. pattern	2. dances with energy.
3. A strong	3. man	3. paints a store.
4. A young	4. fireman	4. thanks a neighbor
5. A known	5. insect	5. wants a sandwich
6. An open	6. notebook	6. sings a song.

Write your *Silly Sentence.*

☐ Starts with capital letter   ☐ Finger spaces between words   ☐ Ends with a punctuation mark

Practice writing your best Nn five times.

Nn

Roll, Highlight, and Write

First List	Second List	Third List
1. His uncle	1. learns numbers	1. on a branch
2. A violin	2. finds a robin	2. downtown.
3. A person	3. sings at night	3. next to land.
4. Her son	4. wins money	4. on a train.
5. That gnome	5. began running	5. at night.
6. This string	6. lands a plane	6. in a nest.

Write your **silly sentence.**

_____

- -

_____

- -

_____

- -

_____

- -

☐ Starts with capital letter   ☐ Finger spaces between words   ☐ Ends with a punctuation mark

Practice writing your best Nn five times.

Make Your Own Sentence

Nn

Who	What	Where
A necklace	irons pants	in a town.
My notebook	joins the navy	in nature.
That nut	changes plans	on the ground.
Her napkin	senses danger	on the plains.
This narwhal	finds a ring	in a barn.
A nurse	sent a note	in the snow.

Write your *silly sentence*.

_____

- -

_____

- -

_____

- -

_____

- -

_____

- -

_____

☐ Starts with capital letter   ☐ Finger spaces between words   ☐ Ends with a punctuation mark

Practice writing your best Nn five times.

Nn

Copy and Draw

Copy your favorite *SILLY SENTENCE* from the Nn pages. Then draw it below.

- -

_____

- -

_____

- -

_____

☐ Starts with capital letter   ☐ Finger spaces between words   ☐ Ends with a punctuation mark

Practice writing your best Nn five times.

Let's Review the Letter

Start with your pencil on the starting dot

Keep O between the <u>top</u> line and <u>bottom</u> line.

<u>Top</u> line ———►

<u>Bottom</u> line ———►

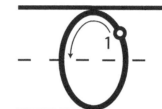

Keep o between the <u>middle</u> line and <u>bottom</u> line.

<u>Middle</u> line ———►

<u>Bottom</u> line ———►

Trace It

Try It

You Can Do It!

Roll, Highlight, and Write

First List	Second List	Third List
1. An ordinary	1. owl	1. opens a door.
2. An original	2. orange	2. observes an object.
3. An opposite	3. ostrich	3. organizes shoes.
4. An old	4. oven	4. outgrew clothes.
5. An odd	5. omelet	5. occupied an office.
6. The only	6. octopus	6. ordered food.

Write your *silly sentence.*

_____

_____

_____

_____

_____

_____

☐ Starts with capital letter   ☐ Finger spaces between words   ☐ Ends with a punctuation mark

Practice writing your best Oo five times.

_____

Roll, Highlight, and Write

First List	Second List	Third List
1. A yellow	1. block	1. located tools.
2. The good	2. moon	2. loves books.
3. That lost	3. book	3. offers money.
4. A loud	4. boy	4. knots a rope.
5. The short	5. brother	5. told jokes.
6. This strong	6. moon	6. wore a coat.

Write your **silly sentence.**

‑ ‑

‑ ‑

‑ ‑

‑ ‑

☐ Starts with capital letter   ☐ Finger spaces between words   ☐ Ends with a punctuation mark

Practice writing your best Oo five times.

Roll, Highlight, and Write

First List	Second List	Third List
1. That ox	1. cooks food	1. outside.
2. A cloud	2. located tools	2. in the morning.
3. My coat	3. told a story	3. through a fog.
4. A person	4. zooms to work	4. on a log.
5. This rose	5. chopped wood	5. on a jog.
6. A foot	6. woke a fox	6. in a pool.

Write your *silly sentence*.

_____

- -

_____

- -

_____

- -

_____

- -

_____

☐ Starts with capital letter   ☐ Finger spaces between words   ☐ Ends with a punctuation mark

Practice writing your best Oo five times.

_____

Make Your Own Sentence

Oo

Who	What	Where
An otter	mops the floor	at the Olympics
The octagon	stood on a box	at a zoo.
This orange	moos loudly	on a boat.
An olive	counts money	in an ocean.
The oatmeal	looks at the moon	on a cot.
That onion	cooks an omelet	at a job.

Write your **silly sentence.**

_____

- -

_____

- -

_____

- -

_____

- -

_____

- -

_____

☐ Starts with capital letter   ☐ Finger spaces between words   ☐ Ends with a punctuation mark

Practice writing your best Oo five times.

Oo

Copy and Draw

Copy your favorite **Silly Sentence** from the Oo pages. Then draw it below.

☐ Starts with capital letter   ☐ Finger spaces between words   ☐ Ends with a punctuation mark

Practice writing your best Oo five times.

Let's Review the Letter

Pp

Start with your pencil on the starting dot

Keep P between the <u>top</u> line and <u>bottom</u> line.

<u>Top</u> line →

<u>Bottom</u> line →

Keep p between the <u>middle</u> line and <u>a little passed the bottom</u> line.

<u>Middle</u> line →

<u>A little passed the bottom</u> line →

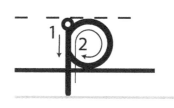

Trace It

Try It

You Can Do It!

Roll, Highlight, and Write

First List	Second List	Third List
1. A perfect	1. page	1. paints a picture.
2. This pretty	2. pear	2. put on pajamas.
3. That pink	3. plane	3. picked a pet.
4. My patient	4. picture	4. plans a party.
5. A powerful	5. pig	5. plays the piano.
6. A peaceful	6. parent	6. paid for a potato.

Write your *silly sentence.*

☐ Starts with capital letter   ☐ Finger spaces between words   ☐ Ends with a punctuation mark

Practice writing your best Pp five times.

Roll, Highlight, and Write

First List	Second List	Third List
1. My happy	1. poem	1. helps a group.
2. That sharp	2. map	2. spots a paw print.
3. A simple	3. pencil	3. paints a pumpkin.
4. Our speedy	4. piano	4. opens a present.
5. A patriotic	5. pan	5. naps on a plane.
6. This peach	6. pumpkin	6. points on a map.

Write your **Silly Sentence.**

_____

- -

_____

- -

_____

- -

_____

- -

_____

☐ Starts with capital letter   ☐ Finger spaces between words   ☐ Ends with a punctuation mark

Practice writing your best Pp five times.

Roll, Highlight, and Write

First List	Second List	Third List
1. My pizza	1. picks up a pen	1. on a ship.
2. A sheep	2. shops for pears	2. at a shop.
3. This rope	3. speaks to people	3. at a party.
4. A peacock	4. played jump rope	4. in paradise.
5. That pen	5. picks up a pen	5. at a picnic.
6. A puppet	6. packed a cap	6. at a parade.

Write your *Silly Sentence.*

☐ Starts with capital letter   ☐ Finger spaces between words   ☐ Ends with a punctuation mark

Practice writing your best Pp five times.

Make Your Own Sentence

Pp

Who	What	Where
Our planet	pulled a rope	in space.
The princess	practices piano	in Europe.
That person	prepares a poem	at a party.
A president	dipped a chip	on a trip.
This puzzle	packed a present	at a park.
A pentagon	helps a pony	at camp.

Write your **silly sentence**.

_____

- -

_____

- -

_____

- -

_____

- -

_____

☐ Starts with capital letter   ☐ Finger spaces between words   ☐ Ends with a punctuation mark

Practice writing your best Pp five times.

Pp

Copy and Draw

Copy your favorite *Silly Sentence* from the Pp pages. Then draw it below.

- [ ] Starts with capital letter
- [ ] Finger spaces between words
- [ ] Ends with a punctuation mark

Practice writing your best Pp five times.

Qq # Let's Review the Letter

Start with your pencil on the starting dot

Keep Q between the <u>top</u> line and <u>bottom</u> line.

<u>Top</u> line ➡️

<u>Bottom</u> line ➡️

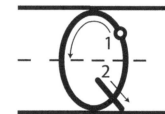

Keep q between the <u>middle</u> line and <u>a little passed the bottom</u> line.

<u>Middle</u> line ➡️

<u>A little passed the bottom</u> line ➡️

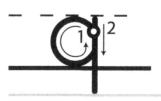

Trace It   Try It

Qq   You Can Do It!

Roll, Highlight, and Write

First List	Second List	Third List
1. A Queen	1. quit	1. quite quickly.
2. My quilt	2. quacked	2. quite loudly.
3. The quail	3. squeaked	3. quite hungrily.
4. That squid	4. squished	4. quite quietly.
5. A squirrel	5. squashed	5. quite sleepily.
6. A square	6. squatted	6. quite happily.

Write your *Silly Sentence*.

_____

- -

_____

- -

_____

- -

_____

- -

_____

☐ Starts with capital letter   ☐ Finger spaces between words   ☐ Ends with a punctuation mark

Practice writing your best Qq five times.

Roll, Highlight, and Write

First List	Second List	Third List
1. A Queen	1. quit	1. quite quickly.
2. My quilt	2. quacked	2. quite loudly.
3. The quail	3. squeaked	3. quite hungrily.
4. That squid	4. squished	4. quite quietly.
5. A squirrel	5. squashed	5. quite sleepily.
6. A square	6. squatted	6. quite happily.

Write your **Silly Sentence.**

☐ Starts with capital letter   ☐ Finger spaces between words   ☐ Ends with a punctuation mark

Practice writing your best Qq five times.

Qq

Roll, Highlight, and Write

First List	Second List	Third List
1. A Queen	1. quit	1. quite quickly.
2. My quilt	2. quacked	2. quite loudly.
3. The quail	3. squeaked	3. quite hungrily.
4. That squid	4. squished	4. quite quietly.
5. A squirrel	5. squashed	5. quite sleepily.
6. A square	6. squatted	6. quite happily.

Write your **silly sentence.**

☐ Starts with capital letter ☐ Finger spaces between words ☐ Ends with a punctuation mark

Practice writing your best Qq five times.

Make Your Own Sentence

Qq

Who	What	Where
A queen	quit	on the queen's throne.
My quilt	quacked	in the queen's car.
The quail	squeaked	over the queen's crown.
That squid	squished	through the queen's yard.
A squirrel	squashed	outside the queen's palace.
A square	squatted	under the queen's bed.

Write your **silly sentence**.

☐ Starts with capital letter   ☐ Finger spaces between words   ☐ Ends with a punctuation mark

Practice writing your best Qq five times.

Qq

Copy and Draw

Copy your favorite *SiLLY Sentence* from the Qq pages. Then draw it below.

- -
_____

_____
- -
_____

_____
- -
_____

☐ Starts with capital letter   ☐ Finger spaces between words   ☐ Ends with a punctuation mark

Practice writing your best Qq five times.

R r

Let's Review the Letter

Start with your pencil on the starting dot

Keep R between the top line and bottom line.

Top line ——————→

Bottom line ——————→

Keep r between the middle line and bottom line.

Middle line ——————→
Bottom line ——————→

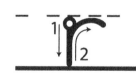

Trace It   Try It

R r   - - - - - - - -   You Can Do It!

Roll, Highlight, and Write

First List	Second List	Third List
1. A ready	1. rainbow	1. races a car.
2. Our real	2. rabbit	2. reads a paper.
3. A royal	3. ring	3. records results.
4. Her red	4. robin	4. repeats a parrot.
5. A reasonable	5. rock	5. rides a rhino.
6. The rich	6. ruler	6. receives a reward.

Write your _silly sentence._

_____

- -

_____

- -

_____

- -

_____

- -

☐ Starts with capital letter   ☐ Finger spaces between words   ☐ Ends with a punctuation mark

Practice writing your best Rr five times.

Rr -

Roll, Highlight, and Write

First List	Second List	Third List
1. An early	1. ear	1. reached for the stars
2. A warm	2. paper	2. marched in a group.
3. A fair	3. rose	3. receives a prize.
4. A great	4. girl	4. rushed to brunch.
5. A green	5. bear	5. grows a flower.
6. A careful	6. farmer	6. travels by train.

Write your **Silly Sentence**.

☐ Starts with capital letter   ☐ Finger spaces between words   ☐ Ends with a punctuation mark

Practice writing your best Rr five times.

Roll, Highlight, and Write

First List	Second List	Third List
1. My doctor	1. ran around	1. near a door
2. A desert	2. heard a bark	2. over there.
3. A teacher	3. wrote a story	3. near the road
4. Her father	4. drives a car	4. far from here.
5. A picture	5. rolls a carpet	5. near a river
6. His letter	6. rules a region	6. under a tree.

Write your *silly sentence.*

_____

- - - - - - - - - - - - - - - - -

_____

- - - - - - - - - - - - - - - - -

_____

- - - - - - - - - - - - - - - - -

_____

- - - - - - - - - - - - - - - - -

_____

☐ Starts with capital letter   ☐ Finger spaces between words   ☐ Ends with a punctuation mark

Practice writing your best Rr five times.

Rr

Rr Make Your Own Sentence

Who	What	Where
The dessert	programs a robot	over here.
A heart	learns to rhyme	on a branch.
Our mother	creates crafts	in a room.
A bird	irons a dress	in a stream.
The horse	wears a zipper	on the street.
His car	raced a rat	over a bridge.

Write your **silly sentence.**

☐ Starts with capital letter   ☐ Finger spaces between words   ☐ Ends with a punctuation mark

Practice writing your best Rr five times.

Rr

Copy and Draw

Copy your favorite *Silly Sentence* from the Rr pages. Then draw it below.

☐ Starts with capital letter ☐ Finger spaces between words ☐ Ends with a punctuation mark

Practice writing your best Rr five times.

S s Let's Review the Letter

Start with your pencil on the starting dot

Keep S between the <u>top</u> line and <u>bottom</u> line.

<u>Top</u> line ⟶

<u>Bottom</u> line ⟶

Keep s between the <u>middle</u> line and <u>bottom</u> line.

<u>Middle</u> line ⟶

<u>Bottom</u> line ⟶

Trace It

Try It

You Can Do It!

Roll, Highlight, and Write

First List	Second List	Third List
1. A safe	1. sandcastle	1. sat on a sofa.
2. A strong	2. Santa Claus	2. sings slowly.
3. A shy	3. sheep	3. saw a seesaw.
4. A sad	4. sun	4. says sorry.
5. A small	5. stick	5. serves sandwiches
6. A soft	6. squirrel	6. soars in the sky.

Write your *Silly Sentence.*

☐ Starts with capital letter ☐ Finger spaces between words ☐ Ends with a punctuation mark

Practice writing your best Ss five times.

Ss

Roll, Highlight, and Write

First List	Second List	Third List
1. A stretchy	1. nest	1. visits in summer
2. A silver	2. insect	2. passed a class.
3. An easy	3. son	3. chose six fish
4. The last	4. string	4. goes to school
5. A famous	5. snake	5. saves a seal.
6. The best	6. shoe	6. sees a soda.

Write your **silly sentence.**

_____

_____

_____

_____

_____

☐ Starts with capital letter   ☐ Finger spaces between words   ☐ Ends with a punctuation mark

Practice writing your best Ss five times.

Ss _____

Roll, Highlight, and Write

First List	Second List	Third List
1. My ear	1. sleeps silently	1. across a shop
2. My scissors	2. plants a seed	2. inside a sink
3. A horse	3. goes outside	3. on the grass
4. The storm	4. makes soap	4. in the sky.
5. My sandals	5. plays music	5. in space.
6. A sandwich	6. ties shoes	6. in the forest

Write your *Silly Sentence.*

☐ Starts with capital letter   ☐ Finger spaces between words   ☐ Ends with a punctuation mark

Practice writing your best Ss five times.

Ss

Make Your Own Sentence

Ss

Who	What	Where
A sock	stops speeders	by the seashore
Santa Claus	sounds a siren	in a shed.
His nose	sells seashells	on a shelf.
Her sister	speaks softly	on the coast.
My sweater	starts sewing	in space.
A soldier	smells soil	in the sea.

Write your **Silly Sentence.**

_____

- -

_____

- -

_____

- -

_____

- -

_____

- -

_____

☐ Starts with capital letter   ☐ Finger spaces between words   ☐ Ends with a punctuation mark

Practice writing your best Ss five times.

Ss -

Copy and Draw

Copy your favorite *Silly Sentence* from the Ss pages. Then draw it below.

_____

- -

_____

_____

- -

_____

_____

- -

_____

☐ Starts with capital letter   ☐ Finger spaces between words   ☐ Ends with a punctuation mark

Practice writing your best Ss five times.

Let's Review the Letter

Start with your pencil on the starting dot

Keep T between the top line and bottom line.

Top line   →

Bottom line   →

Keep t between the top line and bottom line.

Top line   →

Bottom line   →

Trace It   Try It

You Can Do It!

Roll, Highlight, and Write

First List	Second List	Third List
1. A tall	1. table	1. takes a test.
2. A trusted	2. teacher	2. talks tiredly.
3. A tidy	3. team	3. thanks a waiter.
4. A talented	4. tooth	4. took a seat.
5. A tiny	5. tiger	5. tidies a tent.
6. A top	6. toy	6. travels by train.

Write your **silly sentence.**

_____

- - - - - - - - - - - - - - - - - - -

_____

- - - - - - - - - - - - - - - - - - -

_____

- - - - - - - - - - - - - - - - - - -

_____

- - - - - - - - - - - - - - - - - - -

_____

☐ Starts with capital letter   ☐ Finger spaces between words   ☐ Ends with a punctuation mark

Practice writing your best Tt five times.

Roll, Highlight, and Write

First List	Second List	Third List
1. A quiet	1. tablet	1. waits patiently.
2. A great	2. mother	2. wants a kitty.
3. The late	3. cat	3. eats tomatoes.
4. The next	4. president	4. watches T.V.
5. A bright	5. sister	5. catches a t-ball.
6. The best	6. brother	6. took a trip.

Write your **Silly Sentence.**

☐ Starts with capital letter   ☐ Finger spaces between words   ☐ Ends with a punctuation mark

Practice writing your best Tt five times.

Roll, Highlight, and Write

First List	Second List	Third List
1. That nest	1. wrote a note	1. at a party.
2. A father	2. takes a picture	2. past midnight.
3. My tea	3. lost a hat	3. on a planet.
4. This tree	4. puts on a coat	4. at a meeting.
5. A light	5. tried a turnip	5. in a stream.
6. That toad	6. gets ketchup	6. on a street.

Write your **Silly Sentence.**

☐ Starts with capital letter   ☐ Finger spaces between words   ☐ Ends with a punctuation mark

Practice writing your best Tt five times.

Make Your Own Sentence

Who	What	Where
A student	lifted weights	from the East.
The train	plants a plant	in the desert.
His t-shirt	switched clothes	on the Earth.
My toe	touched a tree	in this weather.
Our T.V.	studied today	on a boat.
That turtle	left a note	through the town.

Write your **silly sentence.**

☐ Starts with capital letter   ☐ Finger spaces between words   ☐ Ends with a punctuation mark

Practice writing your best Tt five times.

Copy and Draw

Copy your favorite **SILLY SENTENCE** from the Tt pages. Then draw it below.

☐ Starts with capital letter   ☐ Finger spaces between words   ☐ Ends with a punctuation mark

Practice writing your best Tt five times.

Ūu **Let's Review the Letter**

Start with your pencil on the starting dot

Keep U between the <u>top</u> line and <u>bottom</u> line.

<u>Top</u> line ➔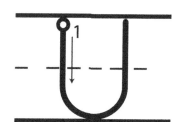

<u>Bottom</u> line ➔

Keep u between the <u>middle</u> line and <u>bottom</u> line.

<u>Middle</u> line ➔

<u>Bottom</u> line ➔

Trace It   Try It

You Can Do It!

Roll, Highlight, and Write

First List	Second List	Third List
1. A useful	1. umpire	1. underlines a number
2. A unique	2. unicorn	2. unfolds underwear
3. An upbeat	3. ukulele	3. uncovers a clue.
4. An upset	4. umbrella	4. unloads a truck
5. An unkind	5. uniform	5. unwraps a burrito
6. An urgent	6. unicycle	6. unpacks a suitcase

Write your Silly Sentence.

_____

- -

_____

- -

_____

- -

_____

- -

_____

☐ Starts with capital letter   ☐ Finger spaces between words   ☐ Ends with a punctuation mark

Practice writing your best Uu five times.

Uu

Roll, Highlight, and Write

First List	Second List	Third List
1. An unaware	1. doughnut	1. uses an umbrella
2. An unfair	2. underwear	2. unrolls a rug
3. An unhappy	3. universe	3. upholds the truth.
4. A cute	4. cub	4. unboxes boxes.
5. A grumpy	5. juice	5. quacks like a duck
6. A busy	6. emu	6. dunks a doughnut.

Write your *Silly Sentence.*

☐ Starts with capital letter   ☐ Finger spaces between words   ☐ Ends with a punctuation mark

Practice writing your best Uu five times.

Uu

Roll, Highlight, and Write

First List	Second List	Third List
1. His uncle	1. struck a puck	1. during a quiz
2. My mug	2. dumps a bucket	2. in a house
3. A bug	3. hugs a pug	3. in a bush
4. The drum	4. jumps to music	4. underground
5. Our fruit	5. upsets a skunk	5. on a route
6. Her bunny	6. hums a tune	6. during lunch

Write your _silly sentence._

_____

- - - - - - - - - - - - - - - - - - -

_____

- - - - - - - - - - - - - - - - - - -

_____

- - - - - - - - - - - - - - - - - - -

_____

- - - - - - - - - - - - - - - - - - -

_____

☐ Starts with capital letter   ☐ Finger spaces between words   ☐ Ends with a punctuation mark

Practice writing your best Uu five times.

Uu _____

Uu Make Your Own Sentence

Who	What	Where
A nurse	pours juice	underground.
That turkey	slurps soup	under a truck.
This duck	uploads a picture	around a house
The brush	uses a menu	in the universe.
A mouse	tunes a guitar	on Uranus.
The queen	cures a virus	under a bush.

Write your **Silly Sentence.**

☐ Starts with capital letter   ☐ Finger spaces between words   ☐ Ends with a punctuation mark

Practice writing your best Uu five times.

Uu

Copy and Draw

Copy your favorite *Silly Sentence* from the Uu pages. Then draw it below.

☐ Starts with capital letter   ☐ Finger spaces between words   ☐ Ends with a punctuation mark

Practice writing your best Uu five times.

Vv # Let's Review the Letter

Start with your pencil on the starting dot

Keep V between the <u>top</u> line and <u>bottom</u> line.

<u>Top</u> line ⟶

<u>Bottom</u> line ⟶

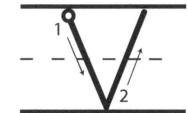

Keep v between the <u>middle</u> line and <u>bottom</u> line.

<u>Middle</u> line ⟶

<u>Bottom</u> line ⟶

Trace It

Try It

You Can Do It!

Roll, Highlight, and Write

First List	Second List	Third List
1. The vast	1. vest	1. views a video.
2. A vacant	2. vase	2. vows to love.
3. A vintage	3. veil	3. voted for a veteran.
4. A vivid	4. violin	4. visits a cave.
5. A valued	5. vine	5. verified a voucher.
6. The vocal	6. visitor	6. vacuums a van.

Write your *silly sentence*.

☐ Starts with capital letter   ☐ Finger spaces between words   ☐ Ends with a punctuation mark

Practice writing your best Vv five times.

Roll, Highlight, and Write

First List	Second List	Third List
1. The heavy	1. vault	1. dives into lava.
2. A velvet	2. vacuum	2. lives in a tavern.
3. My favorite	3. video	3. saves lives.
4. That lively	4. van	4. receives an oven.
5. Her savvy	5. vase	5. lives with leaves.
6. His brave	6. vehicle	6. discovers silver.

Write your **Silly Sentence.**

_____

- -

_____

- -

_____

- -

_____

- -

_____

- -

_____

☐ Starts with capital letter   ☐ Finger spaces between words   ☐ Ends with a punctuation mark

Practice writing your best Vv five times.

Roll, Highlight, and Write

First List	Second List	Third List
1. A vessel	1. vacuums	1. with a violin
2. A cave	2. drives	2. above a valley.
3. A villain	3. travels	3. at an event.
4. A vent	4. lives	4. in the evening.
5. A vine	5. votes	5. in a river.
6. A volcano	6. waves	6. at a venue.

Write your **Silly Sentence.**

☐ Starts with capital letter   ☐ Finger spaces between words   ☐ Ends with a punctuation mark

Practice writing your best Vv five times.

Make Your Own Sentence

Who	What	Where
A vest	volunteers	on a voyage.
A vaccine	drives	in a vault.
A vegetable	vanishes	in a vehicle.
A vulture	votes	in a cave.
A vitamin	lives	in a village.
A vine	moves	on a vessel.

Write your *silly sentence.*

☐ Starts with capital letter   ☐ Finger spaces between words   ☐ Ends with a punctuation mark

Practice writing your best Vv five times.

Copy and Draw

Copy your favorite **Silly Sentence** from the Vv pages. Then draw it below.

☐ Starts with capital letter   ☐ Finger spaces between words   ☐ Ends with a punctuation mark

Practice writing your best Vv five times.

Let's Review the Letter

Start with your pencil on the starting dot

Keep W between the <u>top</u> line and <u>bottom</u> line.

Top line ⟶

Bottom line ⟶

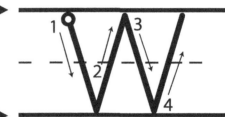

Keep w between the <u>middle</u> line and <u>bottom</u> line.

<u>Middle</u> line ⟶

<u>Bottom</u> line ⟶

Trace It

Try It

You Can Do It!

Roll, Highlight, and Write

First List	Second List	Third List
1. A worried	1. wife	1. wasted water.
2. A wax	2. walrus	2. washes windows.
3. A wonderful	3. wave	3. wishes to win.
4. A wise	4. wheel	4. waves a wand.
5. A warm	5. woman	5. walks wearily.
6. A welcoming	6. wall	6. waits for a waiter.

Write your *Silly Sentence.*

_____

- -

_____

- -

_____

- -

_____

- -

_____

☐ Starts with capital letter   ☐ Finger spaces between words   ☐ Ends with a punctuation mark

Practice writing your best Ww five times.

 # Roll, Highlight, and Write

First List	Second List	Third List
1. A yellow	1. washcloth	1. whiffs waffles.
2. A weepy	2. wheel	2. wipes water.
3. A wet	3. window	3. whispers words.
4. A white	4. wing	4. wants walnuts.
5. A wide	5. wagon	5. watches a whale.
6. A wonky	6. wave	6. washes a wig.

Write your **silly sentence.**

_____

- -

_____

- -

_____

- -

_____

- -

_____

☐ Starts with capital letter   ☐ Finger spaces between words   ☐ Ends with a punctuation mark

Practice writing your best Ww five times.

W w

Roll, Highlight, and Write

First List	Second List	Third List
1. A flower	1. wears a crown	1. below a window
2. A walrus	2. swims slowly	2. while writing.
3. An owl	3. wakes a woman	3. with a flower
4. A fawn	4. sews a gown	4. while yawning.
5. A watch	5. writes words	5. down a well.
6. A jewel	6. howls at a wolf	6. with a wrench.

Write your *silly sentence.*

_____

- -

_____

- -

_____

- -

_____

- -

_____

☐ Starts with capital letter   ☐ Finger spaces between words   ☐ Ends with a punctuation mark

Practice writing your best Ww five times.

Make Your Own Sentence

Who	What	Where
A macaw	mows the lawn	below a rainbow.
A pillow	washes a towel	between the crowd.
A waffle	floats on water	downtown.
The jewel	went to work	with two waffles.
My wagon	plows the snow	in a town.
A whale	draws a cow	below a wall.

Write your **silly sentence**.

_____

- -

_____

- -

_____

- -

_____

- -

_____

- -

☐ Starts with capital letter ☐ Finger spaces between words ☐ Ends with a punctuation mark

Practice writing your best Ww five times.

Copy and Draw

Copy your favorite **SiLLy SenTence** from the Ww pages. Then draw it below.

- -

_____

- -

_____

- -

_____

☐ Starts with capital letter   ☐ Finger spaces between words   ☐ Ends with a punctuation mark

Practice writing your best Ww five times.

Let's Review the Letter

Start with your pencil on the starting dot ✏️

Keep X between the <u>top</u> line and <u>bottom</u> line.

<u>Top</u> line ➡️

<u>Bottom</u> line ➡️

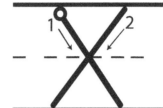

Keep x between the <u>middle</u> line and <u>bottom</u> line.

<u>Middle</u> line ➡️
<u>Bottom</u> line ➡️

Trace It   Try It

You Can Do It!

Roll, Highlight, and Write

First List	Second List	Third List
1. An ox	1. unboxed	1. six meatballs.
2. A box	2. fixed	2. six laptops.
3. A fox	3. mixed	3. six lightbulbs.
4. An x-ray	4. flexed	4. six elephants.
5. A xylophone	5. relaxed with	5. six bathtubs.
6. A taxi	6. exercised with	6. six airplanes.

Write your **silly sentence.**

_____

- -
_____

- -
_____

- -
_____

- -
_____

- -
_____

☐ Starts with capital letter   ☐ Finger spaces between words   ☐ Ends with a punctuation mark

Practice writing your best Xx five times.

Roll, Highlight, and Write

First List	Second List	Third List
1. An ox	1. unboxed	1. six meatballs
2. A box	2. fixed	2. six laptops
3. A fox	3. mixed	3. six lightbulbs
4. An x-ray	4. flexed	4. six elephants
5. A xylophone	5. relaxed with	5. six bathtubs
6. A taxi	6. exercised with	6. six airplanes

Write your *Silly Sentence*.

_____

- -

_____

- -

_____

- -

_____

- -

_____

- -

☐ Starts with capital letter   ☐ Finger spaces between words   ☐ Ends with a punctuation mark

Practice writing your best Xx five times.

Roll, Highlight, and Write

First List
1. An ox
2. A box
3. A fox
4. An x-ray
5. A xylophone
6. A taxi

Second List
1. boxed
2. exceled
3. texted
4. flexed
5. relaxed
6. exercised

Third List
1. next to a T-Rex.
2. next to the galaxy.
3. next to a sandbox.
4. next to a mailbox.
5. next to a lunchbox.
6. next to Texas.

Write your **Silly Sentence**.

_____

_____

_____

_____

_____

_____

☐ Starts with capital letter   ☐ Finger spaces between words   ☐ Ends with a punctuation mark

Practice writing your best Xx five times.

Make Your Own Sentence

Xx

Who	What	Where
An ox	boxed	next to a T-Rex.
A box	exceled	next to a galaxy.
A fox	texted	next to a sandbox.
An x-ray	flexed	next to a mailbox.
A xylophone	relaxed	next to a lunchbox.
A taxi	exercised	next to Texas.

Write your silly sentence.

_____

- -

_____

- -

_____

- -

_____

- -

_____

- -

☐ Starts with capital letter   ☐ Finger spaces between words   ☐ Ends with a punctuation mark

Practice writing your best Xx five times.

Xx

Copy and Draw

Copy your favorite **Silly Sentence** from the Xx pages. Then draw it below.

‒ ‒

‒ ‒

‒ ‒

☐ Starts with capital letter   ☐ Finger spaces between words   ☐ Ends with a punctuation mark

Practice writing your best Xx five times.

Y y # Let's Review the Letter

Start with your pencil on the starting dot

Keep Y between the <u>top</u> line and <u>bottom</u> line.

<u>Top</u> line ———▶

<u>Bottom</u> line ———▶

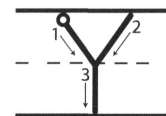

Keep y between the <u>middle</u> line and <u>a little</u>
<u>passed the bottom</u> line.

<u>Middle</u> line ———▶

<u>A little passed</u>
<u>the bottom</u> line ———▶

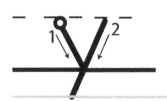

Trace It

Try It

You Can Do It!

Roll, Highlight, and Write

First List	Second List	Third List
1. A yellow	1. yam	1. yanks a toy.
2. A yummy	2. yarn	2. yelps at a pony.
3. A youthful	3. yogurt	3. yaps at a boy.
4. A yelling	4. yacht	4. yodeled yesterday.
5. A young	5. yak	5. annoys everybody.
6. A yawning	6. kitty	6. sprays everyone.

Write your *Silly Sentence.*

_____

- -

_____

- -

_____

- -

_____

- -

_____

☐ Starts with capital letter   ☐ Finger spaces between words   ☐ Ends with a punctuation mark

Practice writing your best Yy five times.

Roll, Highlight, and Write

Yy

First List	Second List	Third List
1. A sneezy	1. pony	1. plays with a yo-yo
2. A cozy	2. toy	2. says "yippee."
3. A wonky	3. key	3. yawns loudly.
4. A foggy	4. baby	4. yells slowly.
5. A jolly	5. yolk	5. surveys the sky
6. A fluffy	6. donkey	6. displays a trophy.

Write your **silly sentence**.

☐ Starts with capital letter   ☐ Finger spaces between words   ☐ Ends with a punctuation mark

Practice writing your best Yy five times.

Yy

Roll, Highlight, and Write

Yy

First List	Second List	Third List
1. A lady	1. pays	1. on a yacht
2. A family	2. yells	2. in a yard
3. A kitty	3. plays	3. at a birthday party
4. A yeti	4. yawns	4. at a gym
5. An army	5. stays	5. on a highway
6. A boy	6. yaps	6. in a city

Write your *Silly Sentence*.

_____

_____

_____

_____

_____

☐ Starts with capital letter ☐ Finger spaces between words ☐ Ends with a punctuation mark

Practice writing your best Yy five times.

Yy

Make Your Own Sentence

Yy

Who	What	Where
A baby	pays	on a yacht.
A pony	yells	in a yard.
A toy	plays	at a birthday party.
A key	yawns	at a gym.
A yolk	stays	on a highway.
A donkey	yaps	in a city.

Write your **Silly Sentence.**

_____

- -

_____

_____

- -

_____

_____

- -

_____

_____

- -

_____

☐ Starts with capital letter   ☐ Finger spaces between words   ☐ Ends with a punctuation mark

Practice writing your best Yy five times.

Yy

Copy and Draw

Yy

Copy your favorite *Silly Sentence* from the Yy pages. Then draw it below.

☐ Starts with capital letter   ☐ Finger spaces between words   ☐ Ends with a punctuation mark

Practice writing your best Yy five times.

Yy Yy

Zz # Let's Review the Letter

Start with your pencil on the starting dot

Keep Z between the top line and bottom line.

Top line ⟶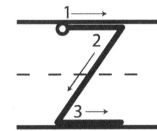

Bottom line ⟶

Keep z between the middle line and bottom line.

Middle line ⟶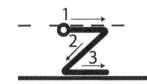
Bottom line ⟶

Trace It

Try It

Zz

You Can Do It!

Roll, Highlight, and Write

First List	Second List	Third List
1. A zen	1. wizard	1. buzzes a buzzer.
2. A zany	2. zebra	2. zips a zipper.
3. A fuzzy	3. puzzle	3. zigzags through a maze.
4. A lazy	4. lizard	4. zooms to a prize.
5. A crazy	5. pizza	5. zaps a buzzer.
6. A frozen	6. zipper	6. zoned out.

Write your *Silly Sentence*.

☐ Starts with capital letter   ☐ Finger spaces between words   ☐ Ends with a punctuation mark

Practice writing your best Zz five times.

Roll, Highlight, and Write

Zz

First List	Second List	Third List
1. A zen	1. wizard	1. buzzes a buzzer.
2. A zany	2. zebra	2. zips a zipper.
3. A fuzzy	3. puzzle	3. zigzags through a maze
4. A lazy	4. lizard	4. zooms to a prize.
5. A crazy	5. pizza	5. zaps a buzzer.
6. A frozen	6. zipper	6. zoned out.

Write your *Silly Sentence*.

☐ Starts with capital letter   ☐ Finger spaces between words   ☐ Ends with a punctuation mark

Practice writing your best Zz five times.

Zz Zz

Roll, Highlight, and Write

First List	Second List	Third List
1. A zen	1. wizard	1. buzzes a buzzer.
2. A zany	2. zebra	2. zips a zipper.
3. A fuzzy	3. puzzle	3. zigzags through a maze.
4. A lazy	4. lizard	4. zooms to a prize.
5. A crazy	5. pizza	5. zaps a buzzer.
6. A frozen	6. zipper	6. zoned out.

Write your **Silly Sentence.**

☐ Starts with capital letter ☐ Finger spaces between words ☐ Ends with a punctuation mark

Practice writing your best Zz five times.

Zz Zz

Zz   Make Your Own Sentence

Who	What	Where
A zen	wizard	buzzes a buzzer.
A zany	zebra	zips a zipper.
A fuzzy	puzzle	zigzags through a maze.
A lazy	lizard	zooms to a prize.
A crazy	pizza	zaps a buzzer.
A frozen	zipper	zoned out.

Write your *SiLLY Sentence*.

_____

- -

_____

- -

_____

- -

_____

- -

_____

- -

☐ Starts with capital letter ☐ Finger spaces between words ☐ Ends with a punctuation mark

Practice writing your best Zz five times.

Zz -

Copy and Draw

Zz

Copy your favorite *Silly Sentence* from the Zz pages. Then draw it below.

☐ Starts with capital letter   ☐ Finger spaces between words   ☐ Ends with a punctuation mark

Practice writing your best Zz five times.

Zz Zz

Certificate

Congratulations! You've finished Handwriting Practice Made Fun: Silly Sentences! You did a great job. Visit our website for a downloadable certificate to celebrate your achievement. Join us in the next workbook for more adventures in handwriting.

We hope you enjoyed the workbook.

Please leave us a review.

Made in the USA
Las Vegas, NV
15 February 2024

85840300R00096